to
Ola,
Emily,
Nils Maarten
and to

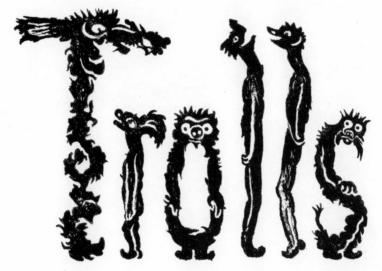

Doubleday & Company, Inc., Garden City, New York

A Zephyr Book

Library of Congress Catalog Card Number 76-158897
Copyright © 1972 by Ingri and Edgar Parin d'Aulaire
All Rights Reserved
Printed in the United States of America

9 8 7 6 5 4 3 2

n the old days, when only narrow, twisting paths wound their way through the moss-grown mountains of Norway, few human beings ever set foot there. The mountains belonged to the trolls, who were as old and moss-grown as the mountains themselves.

There were many kinds of trolls: mountain trolls, forest trolls, water trolls, trolls with one head, trolls with three heads, trolls with twelve heads. Most of them were bachelors and lived by their lonely selves; others had wives, who were as ungainly as their husbands. Some kept cats, large black troll-cats with gleaming eyes. They had troll-cocks too, with green and purple feathers. And in their stables, deep in the mountains, stood their troll-steeds; they were huge and so fierce that flames spurted from their nostrils.

Under the hills lived the hulder-people. They weren't exactly trolls, but were related to them and like the trolls they had no souls. They were not huge and ugly; they looked almost like human beings, and their daughters, the hulder-maidens, were even bewitchingly beautiful.

Smallest of the tribe of trolls were the gnomes. They were little men with glowing amber eyes and cats' whiskers. Some of them mined gold deep in the mountains, some lived in the dark corners of people's barns. They were hot-tempered and mischievous whenever they were crossed, but they were not evil and dangerous like the big trolls.

Biggest and strongest of all the trolls were those who lived inside the mountains. They had the strength of fifty men and they also had great magic powers and could throw spells over people. They hated the smell of human beings, the tinkle of church bells, and most of all they hated the sun. They were creatures of darkness who knew that a mere glimpse of the sun would burst them apart and turn them to stone. So when the sun was up they slept inside their mountains. But as soon as the sun went down, the troll-cocks began to crow.

When the troll-cocks crowed heavy stone doors in the mountain walls creaked open, and the trolls came yawning out. They called to each other across the valleys, and their voices rumbled like thunder from mountain-side to mountainside.

On farms nestled down in the valleys, people turned to each other and said, "Close your doors and windows tightly—the trolls are out tonight." For well they knew that the gluttonous trolls loved tender tasty humans for their stewpots.

So the whole night the trolls had the mountains to themselves. They prowled about in the moonlight casting huge dark shadows, and the troll-children howled and screamed and fought over blueberry patches. The old trolls were gruff and gnarled, and if they had ever washed it must have been very long ago. Flies and moths swarmed around them

and shrubs and weeds sprouted from their noses and ears. Many of them had tails as well, cowtails, pigtails or short, stubby bear tails.

The troll-children weren't much prettier, and the troll-hags were uglier still. They had long, red, crooked noses, and some of them even carried their heads under their arms.

At the first faint light of dawn the trolls shuffled back into their mountains and slammed the stone doors shut behind them. There, inside, no dark, damp caves awaited them, but great halls lit by glittering gold. They sat on chairs of burnished gold at tables of solid silver and stuffed themselves with pig snouts, bear tails and sour cream pudding.

The troll-hags liked to cook and their long, crooked noses came in handy for stirring the stew and raking the embers in the hearth! The young ones crowded around the kettle, burning their fingers, singeing each other's tails, while they waited for the old troll to eat his fill.

The more heads a troll had, the more trouble he had at mealtimes, for all his greedy mouths shouted, "I am hungry. Feed me first. It's my turn!" Since even a many-headed troll had only two hands, he would be a very tired troll before the meal was over.

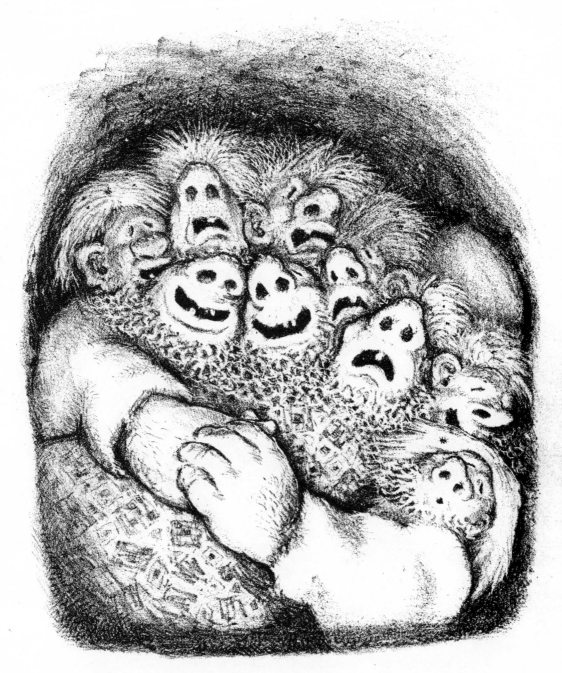

Then he would need a good long nap under his quilt made of squares of silver and squares of gold. Some of his heads had bad dreams, some had happy dreams, some did not dream at all.

The trolls were very, very rich, for they owned all the silver and gold hidden in the mountains. The richest of them were the troll-kings, and every mountain range had its king. He sat on a throne of solid gold while troll-courtiers crowded around him. They bowed and scraped and tied knots in their tails. It hurt, but they did not mind, for the more knots

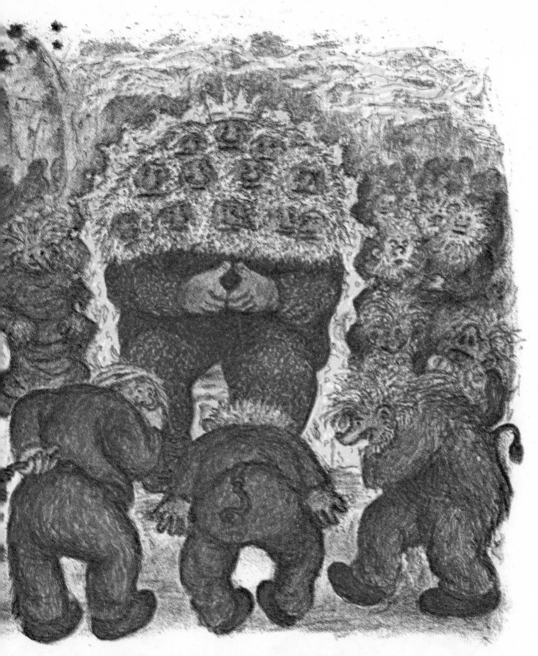

a troll could tie in his tail, the higher became his rank. Those who had ribbons pinned to their knots were the highest of the high.

Other trolls stuffed themselves with food and drink or clomped about with their troll-hags. A loud sound of rumbling and trampling came from the mountain where the troll-king held court.

The clumsy troll-daughters, comely in their fathers' eyes, waddled to the magic melodies of visiting hulder-maidens. The hulder-maidens were beautiful—when seen from the front. But not from behind, for like the trolls, they too, had tails, long cowtails that trailed behind them.

Sometimes even the hard-working gnomes took time off from toiling in the mountains to play in the glittering hall. The little, gray-clad men whirled about so fast that the big, black troll-cats mistook them for balls of gray yarn and pounced on them. That made the gnomes very angry.

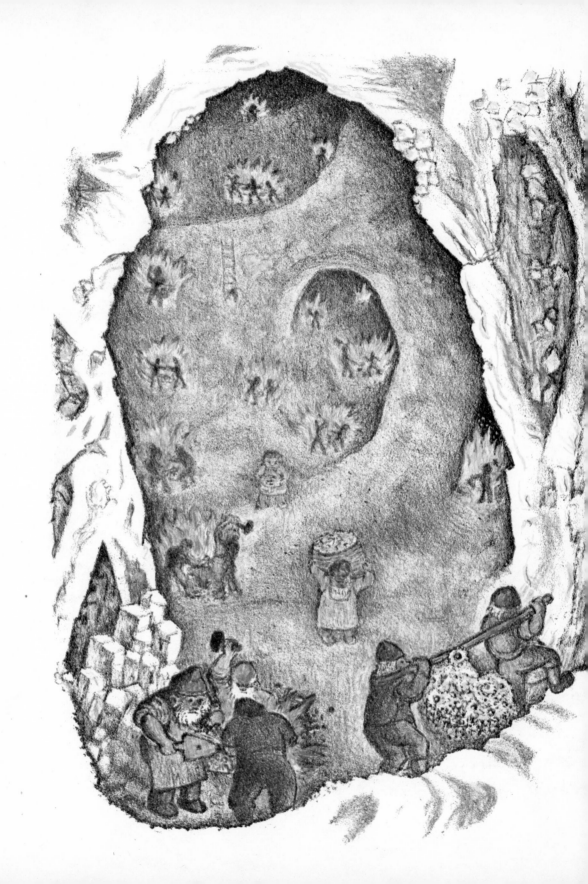

The gnomes knew where the treasures in the ground lay hidden, and it was they who mined the silver and gold for the trolls. They were skilled smiths as well, and busily they swung their small hammers to forge the precious metals into wondrous shapes for the trolls to enjoy.

There was very little a troll could spend his gold on, so he grew richer and richer. He liked just to sit on his pile of treasure and feel it grow under him. The tinkling of gold was music to his ears.

Some mighty trolls even owned golden forests, where the tree trunks were of copper, the twigs were of silver and the leaves were made of the purest gold. These forests were so dense that not a ray of sunshine could creep in; they were lit by the shimmering gold alone. Woe to

anyone, troll or human, who tried to break off as much as a single leaf!
The troll who owned the forest would hear the tinkling of the gold and
rush out bellowing:

"Who dares to touch my trees?"

If the troll did not kill the poor fellow outright, he would cast a spell upon him and turn him into a cat, a bear, a lion or whatever beast came into his mind. There were many strange animals running around in the twilight of the enchanted forest, hoping one day to regain their true shapes.

The more heads a troll had, the wilder and more fearsome he was. A troll with twelve heads was twelve times fiercer and twelve times stronger than a troll with only one head. But a twelve-headed troll had one great weakness. When he grew angry, all his mouths roared right into his twenty-four ears, and that gave him twelve splitting headaches. Then it was hard for him to keep his wits together.

All he could do was to sit down and scratch his aching, shaggy heads. Trolls liked to have their heads scratched, even without headaches. For their messy hair was full of burrs, beetles and berries, and birds built nests behind their ears. Best of all they liked to have the scratching done by the gentle little hands of human princesses.

There once was a troll with twelve heads who searched far and wide for a king who had twelve daughters, one maiden for each head. When at last he found such a king, he came raging along, swinging his huge troll-sword. "Give me your twelve daughters or I will destroy your whole kingdom," he bellowed. The king wept and wrung his hands, but much as he hated to give his twelve daughters to a troll, he had to do it to save his kingdom.

The king's daughters cried and carried on as the troll tucked them under his arms and strode off with them, but not even the bravest of the king's men dared come to their rescue. Who could fight a troll with twelve heads?

The troll took the princesses to his faraway mountain and swung the great stone door closed behind him. The maidens wept and sobbed and sobbed and wept, and never expected to see the light of day again.

But a brave young lad had watched the troll and had seen which way he went. He followed through dense forests and deep, dark valleys until at last he came to a steep mountain where he heard a rumble of snoring from within.

"Aha," he thought, "so this is where the princesses are hidden, scratching away at the sleeping troll's heads!"

The lad was young, but he knew just what to do, for he had listened well when old people spoke of how to do away with trolls.

He crept in through a crack in the mountain, looked around and sure enough, there were the twelve princesses scratching the sleeping troll's ugly heads. Behind the big stone door stood the troll's huge sword and next to it hung the troll's magic flask. He took three gulps from the flask and that made him so strong that he could lift the huge sword. "Move aside," he whispered to the princesses, and swung the sword.

He took good aim, for well he knew that should he miss but one single head, the troll would wake up, put the other heads back in place and bring them to life with some drops from the magic flask. And then in his troll-rage he would surely make an end to the lad and to the king's daughters too.

The lad swung the sword so well that all the heads flew off at once. Then he ran to the troll's stable and sprinkled some drops from the magic flask on the huge horse. At once it became so tame that he could mount it and, with the king's twelve daughters behind him, he burst out of the stone door and down the steep mountain wall. He rode the horse so fast that sparks flew from its hoofs. He knew he had better be far away before any other trolls arrived. Eleven of the princesses had their hands full, holding onto the silver and gold they had snatched up in the mountain. But the youngest only held onto the lad who had saved them all.

Since the path ran through the troll's enchanted forest, the lad took the time to sprinkle some drops from the magic flask on the bewitched people who roamed around in animal shapes. At once they became human beings again and could not thank him enough.

When he brought the princesses safely home, the king rewarded him richly. He gave him half the kingdom and the youngest and prettiest of his daughters for a bride. And everybody agreed that anyone brave enough to slay a troll with twelve heads and tame a troll-horse was second to no one but the king himself.

Not all big trolls were mountain trolls. Some lived under bridges—big trolls under big bridges, smaller trolls under small bridges. Some lived at the bottom of the sea, and some in deep, dark pools where they frightened away the fish from the fishermen's flies.

The water trolls, too, loved to have their heads scratched. Sometimes, on moonlit nights, they would let their heads bob up and down near the shore. When a pretty girl came walking along they beseeched her to comb their ugly heads, all covered with seaweed, crabs and jellyfish. If she were kind enough to do so, she would be richly rewarded: thereafter gold would drip from her hair whenever she combed it. But if she were cross and snapped, "Troll, scratch yourself," frogs and toads would jump from her mouth whenever she spoke.

There were forest trolls too, who shambled about in the deep, dark shadows of the woods. Some were taller than the tallest pines, some looked like huge ragged tramps, some like scruffy bears. Most of them had only one huge head with a very small brain in it and they could easily be outwitted. But when they grew angry, they would tear up whole stretches of forest and smash the trees into kindling wood.

Once a lumberjack met a forest troll deep in the woods. Scared as he was, he put on a bold face and called out: "Troll, can you squeeze water out of a stone the way I can?" The troll picked up a stone and squeezed it with all his might, but strong as he was, he could barely wring out one single drop. "Now watch me," cried the lumberjack as he reached down for a round, soft cheese that he had hidden among the white stones. He squeezed it and the troll stared in wonder as the whey oozed from between the boy's fingers. "And now I'll squeeze you too," cried the lumberjack.

"No," pleaded the troll, "I'll do whatever you want me to do."

"Then cut this forest for me," said the lumberjack.

In no time at all the forest was cleared and the logs stacked. "That fellow must have a troll working for him," people said. But a lad smart enough to fool a troll was smart enough to keep a secret.

Some of the forest trolls had only one eye set in the middle of their foreheads, and it even happened that three trolls shared a single eye. They took turns looking through it, passing it from one to the other.

One night a young fellow met three such trolls as they stumbled

through the woods, trampling down trees with their big feet. He sneaked up to them and gave the one who was holding the eye a sharp blow on his shin.

"Ouch," howled the troll. "A wasp has stung me!" He grabbed his leg and dropped the eye. Quickly the boy caught it.

While the three blind trolls fell all over each other groping for the eye, the boy called: "It is I who have your eye and I'll only give it back for a pile of silver and gold." First the trolls raged, then they threatened, then they begged, and at last they called to their troll-hag and told her to bring a troughful of silver and gold and give it to him. (They only had one wife between them since they had only one eye to see her with.) She came running, threw the treasure at the boy's feet and grabbed the eye. "Can't three big trolls like you even hold onto one little eye?" she yelled, and led her three husbands back into the mountain and slammed the stone door shut.

Before the boy gave the eye back, he peeked through it and what he saw was very strange. Light was dark, dark was light, and even the raging trolls looked gentle and kind. For trolls had troll-splinters in their eyes and that made them see everything askew.

That is why when a troll looked into his rock-crystal mirror, he was so pleased with what he saw. To his eyes his ungainly wife looked rosy-cheeked and buxom, and the troll-children were the finest of young

fellows, frisky like young cubs as they wrestled and tumbled about.

Only they screamed and yelled from morning to night, and that was just the time when trolls wanted to sleep.

No wonder the troll-hags looked with envy at the good little babies on the farms down in the valleys! *They* did their crying at night and slept peacefully during the days.

Whenever a troll-hag had a chance, she would snatch an infant from his cradle and put one of her troll-brats in his place. Then there was just one way for the mother to get her own child back. She had to take the

ugly changeling behind the barn on a dark Thursday night and spank him soundly. If she was lucky, his howls would melt the stony heart of the troll-hag and she would come running, toss the human child to his mother, grab her own and storm back into the mountain with him. If this did not work, the poor mother had to live for the rest of her life with a troll in her house.

When a child grew up, the troll-hags no longer had power over him. But then he had to beware of the hulder-maidens. For the dream of every hulder-maiden was to get a human boy in her power and have him for her husband. When a young man heard an enticing song and saw a beautiful girl leading a herd of small black cows on the lonely highlands, he had better make sure that one of the cowtails did not belong to her. If it did, he had better take to his heels, for if he let the hulder-maiden come too close, her beauty would bewitch him and he might follow her into her underground world. When that happened, trolls watching from afar opened their huge mouths wide as barn doors and laughed: "Haaa! That fellow will never be seen again."

Then down below, in the twilight of the hulder-world, the bewitched boy was welcomed by the old hulder-people. They were furrowed and faded like old, gray sod, not beautiful like the young maidens. But they were rich and lived in plenty on their underground farms where snow never fell and fat cows grazed on green pastures.

What a wedding feast they spread for him; nowhere else had he tasted

so rich a cream pudding.

For a while the youth would be homesick and search for a way up to his own world. But living in plenty with his hulder-wife, never having to work or worry, he soon forgot that he had ever been a human. And, when at last he died, nothing was left of him but gray sod. He had lost his soul!

Luckier was the young man who kept his head and brought the hulder-maiden home to his people. For when he took her to church and married her, a strange thing happened: the moment the church bells rang over her head, her tail dropped off and she gained an eternal soul like her husband's instead. Her trusted bridesmaid would quickly hide the tail so none of the wedding guests would spot it lying on the church steps.

Angrily the mountain trolls banged their stone doors to drown out the sound of the church bells. They were furious that one of their kin had gone astray.

But the hulder-people had no troll-splinters in their eyes and they were happy that one of their daughters had gained herself a soul. They saw to it that her husband prospered. As long as he treated his wife kindly, his barn was filled with hay and his cows grew sleek and fat.

The gnome who lived up in the hayloft helped too, for the hulder-bride
well knew that the bristling whiskers and glowing amber eyes in the far
corner of the barn did not belong to a cat. Whenever she milked, she
set aside a saucer for the gray-clad gnome, and on holy evenings she
gave him his share of the pudding. In return, the gnome would run to
unfriendly neighbors' barns and whisk away an armful of hay whenever
he thought the cows looked hungry.

The hulder-maiden's fairy beauty soon faded, but she made a good wife. She was husky and strong and bore her husband fine children. Her children were proud of having a hulder-mother, for that made them different from other people. They could see and hear things that were hidden from others. Some of them even understood the language of the birds and the beasts, and they became great storytellers. Even trolls came to listen and sat spellbound all through the night when the hulder-children told their strange tales. Neither trolls nor troll-hags had power over them, so they were not afraid. But they had no love for the uncouth creatures.

Late one night a hulder-lad said to a troll and his hag: "Now I shall tell you the story of the very first trolls, the fearsome frost giants."

"They lived in castles of ice, surrounded by shimmering fences of northern lights. They were as wild as the mountains themselves and pelted the valleys with snow and ice—nobody dared to live in a place near them. They had more gold and silver than they knew what to do with, and hard-working gnomes were forever bringing them more. So when they

were in a good mood, they would playfully toss huge balls of gold to each other. The frost giants were much bigger and stronger than you, plain trolls, and some of them had as many as five hundred heads on their shoulders. What trolls they were!"

"Tell us more," said the trolls, their mouths agape.

"Then churches were built down in the valleys and the fine pealing of the bells hurt their rough ears so badly that they took their vast treasures and moved into the mountains."

"What then, what then?" cried the trolls, and quite forgot to look out for the rising sun.

"Well," said the boy, "don't you know that yourselves? By and by the giants faded into the past and trolls like you took over their mountain halls. You think you have all their treasures, but you are paupers compared to them. The biggest ball of gold they hid behind the mountain yonder."

"Where?" cried the trolls, and spun around. They stared straight into the golden eye of the rising sun.

With a loud crack they burst and turned to stone. One became a mountain, the other a heap of rubble. They had done what no troll must ever do. For trolls were creatures of darkness and just one glance at the sun was enough to destroy them.

Many trolls must have been tricked in this way, for none have been

seen walking around for over a hundred years. Have they all burst or are some still hiding behind their stone doors?

Are the gnomes still mining deep in the mountains?

And are the hulder-people still herding their fat little cows down under the hills? We cannot be certain.

But we do know that every time a troll burst, the splinter in his eye was scattered far and wide. Maybe that is why there are people everywhere today who see things askew. What is bad looks good to them and what is wrong looks right. They do not know that they have troll-splinters in their eyes and you cannot see them. But you can be very sure that the troll-splinters are there.